ANTIGONE

Antigone is one of Anouilh's 'Plays Black' and is based on Sophocles' version of the classical tragedy where the eponymous heroine dies for the crime of offering her dead brother, the rebel Polynices, proper burial rites despite the decree by the king, Creon, that Polynices is to remain unburied and unwept.

JEAN ANOUILH was born in Bordeaux in 1910, but went to Paris when still young, began to study law, then worked for an advertising agency. In 1931 he became secretary to the actor-manager, Louis Jouvet, and his first play, *The Ermine*, was staged the following year. *Antigone* firmly established his popularity in France in 1944, and Peter Brook's 1950 production of *Ring Round the Moon* (1947) in Christopher Fry's translation made his name in England. Of his many other plays, which he himself has categorised as 'Plays Black', 'Plays Pink', 'Plays Bright' etc., the best-known in English are: *Restless Heart* (1934); *Dinner with the Family, Traveller without Luggage* (both 1937); *Thieves Carnival* (1938); *Léocadia* (1939); *Point of Departure* (1941); *Romeo and Jeannette* (1945); *Medea* (1946); *Ardèle* (1948); *The Rehearsal* (1950); *Colombe* (1951); *The Waltz of the Toreadors* (1952); *The Lark* (1953); *Ornifle* (1955); *Poor Bitos* (1956); *Becket* (1959); *The Fighting Cock* (1966); *Dear Antoine* (1971); *The Director of the Opera* (1973); *Number One* (1981).

by the same author

BECKET
THE LARK

ANOUILH PLAYS: ONE
(Antigone, The Lark,
Poor Bitos, Leocadia,
The Waltz of the Toreadors)

Antigone

A TRAGEDY BY
JEAN ANOUILH

Translated by
LEWIS GALANTIÈRE

METHUEN DRAMA

A METHUEN MODERN PLAY

Originally published as Antigone
Copyright © 1951 by Jean Anouilh and Lewis Galantière
First English edition published by Methuen & Co Ltd 1951
First published in this edition 1960
Reprinted seven times
Reprinted 1982, 1985 by Methuen London Ltd

Reprinted in 1989 (twice) by Methuen Drama
an imprint of Reed Consumer Books Ltd
Michelin House, 81 Fulham Road, London SW3 6RB
and Auckland, Melbourne, Singapore and Toronto

Reprinted 1990, 1991 (twice)
Reissued with a new cover design 1994

Printed and bound in Great Britain by
Cox & Wyman Ltd, Reading, Berkshire
ISBN 0 413 30860 X

The photograph on the front cover shows Vivien Leigh as Antigone. It is reproduced by courtesy of Angus McBean, London.

This play was first presented in Great Britain by the Old Vic Theatre Company at the New Theatre, London, on 10th February, 1949, with the following cast:

(*In the order in which they speak*)

CHORUS	Laurence Olivier
ANTIGONE	Vivien Leigh
NURSE	Eileen Beldon
ISMENE	Meg Maxwell
HAEMON	Dan Cunningham
CREON	George Relph
FIRST GUARD (*Jonas*)	Thomas Heathcote
SECOND GUARD (*a Corporal*)	Hugh Stewart
THIRD GUARD	George Cooper
MESSENGER	Terence Morgan
PAGE	Michael Redington
EURYDICE	Helen Beck

Produced by LAURENCE OLIVIER

THE SETTING

A grey cloth cyclorama, semicircular, hangs at the back of
the set. At the bottom of the cyclorama, a stair, of three
steps, sweeps in a semicircle. Downstage, right and left,
two archways. The curtains part in the centre for entrance
and exit.

A table stands left of centre-stage, with matching chairs
set at either end. A small stool is placed right of the chair
at the right of the table.

ANTIGONE

ANTIGONE, *her hands clasped round her knees, sits on the top step. The* THREE GUARDS *sit on the steps, in a small group, playing cards.* CHORUS *stands on the top step.* EURYDICE *sits on the top step, just left of centre, knitting. The* NURSE *sits on the second step, left of* EURYDICE. ISMENE *stands in front of arch, left, facing* HAEMON, *who stands left of her.* CREON *sits in the chair at right end of the table, his arm over the shoulder of his* PAGE, *who sits on the stool beside his chair. The* MESSENGER *is leaning against the downstage portal of the right arch.*

The curtain rises slowly: then CHORUS *turns and moves downstage.*

CHORUS.   Well, here we are.

These people are about to act out for you the story of Antigone.

That thin little creature sitting by herself, staring straight ahead, seeing nothing, is Antigone. She is thinking. She is thinking that the instant I finish telling you who's who and what's what in this play, she will burst forth as the tense, sallow, wilful girl whose family would never take her seriously and who is about to rise up alone against Creon, her uncle, the King.

Another thing that she is thinking is this: she is going to die. Antigone is young. She would much rather live than die. But there is no help for it. When your name is Antigone, there is only one part you can play; and she will have to play hers through to the end.

From the moment the curtain went up, she began to feel that inhuman forces were whirling her out of this world, snatching her away from her sister, Ismene, whom you see smiling and chatting with that young man; from all of us who sit or stand here, looking at her, not in the least upset ourselves—for we are not doomed to die tonight.

CHORUS *turns and indicates* HAEMON.

The young man talking to Ismene—to the gay and beautiful Ismene—is Haemon. He is the King's son, Creon's son. Antigone and he are engaged to be married. You wouldn't have thought she was his type. He likes dancing, sports, competition; he likes women, too. Now look at Ismene again. She is certainly more beautiful than Antigone. She is the girl you'd think he'd go for. Well. . . . There was a ball one night. Ismene wore a new evening frock. She was radiant. Haemon danced every dance with her. And yet, that same night, before the dance was over, suddenly he went in search of Antigone, found her sitting alone—like that, with her arms clasped round her knees—and asked her to marry him. We still don't know how it happened. It didn't seem to surprise Antigone in the least. She looked up at him out of those solemn eyes of hers, smiled sort of sadly and said "yes". That was all. The band struck up another dance. Ismene, surrounded by a group of young men, laughed out loud. And . . . well, here is Haemon expecting to marry Antigone. He won't, of course. He didn't know, when he asked her, that the earth wasn't meant to hold a husband of Antigone, and that this princely distinction was to earn him no more than the right to die sooner than he might otherwise have done.

CHORUS *turns towards* CREON.

That grey-haired, powerfully built man sitting lost in thought, with his little page at his side, is Creon, the King. His face is lined. He is tired. He practises the difficult art of a leader of men. When he was younger, when Oedipus was King and Creon was no more than the King's brother-in-law, he was different. He loved music, bought rare manuscripts, was a kind of art patron. He would while away whole afternoons in the antique shops of this city of Thebes. But Oedipus died. Oedipus' sons died. Creon had to roll up his sleeves and take over the kingdom. Now and then, when he goes to bed weary with the day's work, he wonders whether this business of being a leader of men is worth the trouble. But when he wakes up, the problems are there to be solved; and like a conscientious workman, he does his job.

Creon has a wife, a Queen. Her name is Eurydice. There she sits, the old lady with the knitting, next to the Nurse who brought up the two girls. She will go on knitting all through the play, till the time comes for her to go to her room and die. She is a good woman, a worthy, loving soul. But she is no help to her husband. Creon has to face the music alone. Alone with his page, who is too young to be of any help.

The others? Well, let's see.

He points towards the MESSENGER.

That pale young man leaning against the wall is the Messenger. Later on, he will come running in to announce that Haemon is dead. He has a premonition of catastrophe. That's what he is brooding over. That's why he won't mingle with the others.

As for those three red-faced card players—they are the guards. One smells of garlic, another of beer; but they're not a bad lot. They have wives they are afraid of, kids who

11

are afraid of them; they're bothered by the little day-to-day worries that beset us all. At the same time—they are policemen: eternally innocent, no matter what crimes are committed; eternally indifferent, for nothing that happens can matter to them. They are quite prepared to arrest anybody at all, including Creon himself, should the order be given by a new leader.

That's the lot. Now for the play.

Oedipus, who was the father of the two girls, Antigone and Ismene, had also two sons, Eteocles and Polynices. After Oedipus died, it was agreed that the two sons should share his throne, each to reign over Thebes in alternate years.

Gradually, the lights on the stage have been dimmed.

But when Eteocles, the elder son, had reigned a full year, and time had come for him to step down, he refused to yield up the throne to his younger brother. There was civil war. Polynices brought up allies—six foreign princes; and in the course of the war he and his foreigners were defeated, each in front of one of the seven gates of the city. The two brothers fought, and they killed one another in single combat just outside the city walls. Now Creon is King.

CHORUS *is leaning, at this point, against the left proscenium arch. By now the stage is dark, with only the cyclorama bathed in dark blue. A single spot lights up the face of* CHORUS.

Creon has issued a solemn edict that Eteocles, with whom he had sided, is to be buried with pomp and honours, and that Polynices is to be left to rot. The vultures and the dogs are to bloat themselves on his carcass. Nobody is to go into mourning for him. No gravestone is to be set up in his memory. And above all, any person who

12

attempts to give him religious burial will himself be put to death.

> *While* CHORUS *has been speaking the characters have gone out one by one.* CHORUS *disappears through the left arch.*
>
> *It is dawn, grey and ashen, in a house asleep.* ANTIGONE *steals in from out of doors, through the arch, right. She is carrying her sandals in her hand. She pauses, looking off through the arch, taut, listening, then turns and moves across downstage. As she reaches the table, she sees the* NURSE *approaching through the arch, left. She runs quickly towards the exit. As she reaches the steps, the* NURSE *enters through the arch and stands still when she sees* ANTIGONE.

NURSE. Where have you been?

ANTIGONE. Nowhere. It was beautiful. The whole world was grey when I went out. And now—you wouldn't recognize it. It's like a postcard: all pink, and green and yellow. You'll have to get up earlier, Nurse, if you want to see a world without colour.

NURSE. It was still pitch black when I got up. I went to your room, for I thought you might have flung off your blanket in the night. You weren't there.

ANTIGONE (*comes down the steps*). The garden was lovely. It was still asleep. Have you ever thought how lovely a garden is when it is not yet thinking of men?

NURSE. You hadn't slept in your bed. I couldn't find you. I went to the back door. You'd left it open.

ANTIGONE. The fields were wet. They were waiting for something to happen. The whole world was breathless, waiting. I can't tell you what a roaring noise I seemed to make alone on the road. It bothered me that whatever was waiting, wasn't waiting for me. I took off my sandals and slipped into a field. (*She moves down to the stool and sits.*)

NURSE (*kneels at* ANTIGONE'*s feet to chafe them and put on the sandals*). You'll do well to wash your feet before you go back to bed, Miss.

ANTIGONE. I'm not going back to bed.

NURSE. Don't be a fool! You get some sleep! And me, getting up to see if she hasn't flung off her blanket; and I find her bed cold and nobody in it!

ANTIGONE. Do you think that if a person got up every morning like this, it would be just as thrilling every morning to be the first girl out of doors?

   NURSE *puts* ANTIGONE'*s left foot down, lifts her other foot and chafes it.*

NURSE. Morning my grandmother! It was night. It still is. And now, my girl, you'll stop trying to squirm out of this and tell me what you were up to. Where've you been?

ANTIGONE. That's true. It was still night. There wasn't a soul out of doors but me who thought that it was morning. Don't you think it's marvellous—to be the first person who is aware that it is morning?

NURSE. Oh, my little flibbertigibbet! Just can't imagine what I'm talking about, can she? Go on with you! I know that game. Where have you been, wicked girl?

ANTIGONE (*soberly*). No. Not wicked.

NURSE. You went out to meet someone, didn't you? Deny it if you can.

ANTIGONE. Yes. I went out to meet someone.

NURSE. A lover?

ANTIGONE. Yes, Nurse. Yes, the poor dear. I have a lover.

NURSE (*stands up; bursting out*). Ah, that's very nice now, isn't it? Such goings-on! You, the daughter of a king, running out to meet lovers. And we work our fingers to the

(sarcasm)

14

bone for you, we slave to bring you up like young ladies! (*She sits on chair, right of table.*) You're all alike, all of you. Even you—who never used to stop to primp in front of a looking-glass, or smear your mouth with rouge, or dindle and dandle to make the boys ogle you, and you ogle back. How many times I'd say to myself, "Now that one, now: I wish she was a little more of a coquette— always wearing the same dress, her hair tumbling round her face. One thing's sure," I'd say to myself, "none of the boys will look at her while Ismene's about, all curled and cute and tidy and trim. I'll have this one on my hands for the rest of my life." And now, you see? Just like your sister, after all. Only worse: a hypocrite. Who is the lad? Some little scamp, eh? Somebody you can't bring home and show to your family, and say, "Well, this is him, and I mean to marry him and no other." That's how it is, is it? Answer me!

ANTIGONE (*smiling faintly*). That's how it is. Yes, Nurse.

NURSE. Yes, says she! God save us! I took her when she wasn't that high. I promised her poor mother I'd make a lady of her. And look at her! But don't you go thinking this is the end of this, my young 'un. I'm only your nurse and you can play deaf and dumb with me; I don't count. But your Uncle Creon will hear of this! That, I promise you.

ANTIGONE (*a little weary*). Yes. Creon will hear of this.

NURSE. And we'll hear what he has to say when he finds out that you go wandering alone o' nights. Not to mention Haemon. For the girl's engaged! Going to be married! Going to be married, and she hops out of bed at four in the morning to meet somebody else in a field. Do you know what I ought to do to you? Take you over my knee the way I used to do when you were little.

ANTIGONE. Please, Nurse, I want to be alone.

15

NURSE. And if you so much as speak of it, she says she wants to be alone!

ANTIGONE. Nanny, you shouldn't scold, dear. This isn't a day when you should be losing your temper.

NURSE. Not scold, indeed! Along with the rest of it, I'm to like it. Didn't I promise your mother? What would she say if she was here? "Old Stupid!" That's what she'd call me. "Old Stupid. Not to know how to keep my little girl pure! Spend your life making them behave, watching over them like a mother hen, running after them with mufflers and sweaters to keep them warm, and egg nogs to make them strong; and then at four o'clock in the morning, you who always complained you never could sleep a wink, snoring in your bed and letting them slip out into the bushes." That's what she'd say, your mother. And I'd stand there, dying of shame if I wasn't dead already. And all I could do would be not to dare look her in the face; and "That's true," I'd say. "That's all true what you say, Your Majesty."

ANTIGONE. Nanny, dear. Dear Nanny. Don't cry. You'll be able to look Mamma in the face when it's your time to see her. And she'll say, "Good morning, Nanny. Thank you for my little Antigone. You did look after her so well." She knows why I went out this morning.

NURSE. Not to meet a lover?

ANTIGONE. No. Not to meet a lover.

NURSE. Well, you've a queer way of teasing me, I must say! Not to know when she's teasing me! (*Rises to stand behind* ANTIGONE.) I must be getting awfully old, that's what it is. But if you loved me, you'd tell me the truth. You'd tell me why your bed was empty when I went along to tuck you in. Wouldn't you?

ANTIGONE. Please, Nanny, don't cry any more. (ANTIGONE *turns partly towards* NURSE, *puts an arm up to* NURSE'S

16

shoulder. With her other hand, ANTIGONE *caresses* NURSE'S *face.*). There now, my sweet red apple. Do you remember how I used to rub your cheeks to make them shine? My dear, wrinkled red apple! I didn't do anything tonight that was worth sending tears down the little gullies of your dear face. I am pure, and I swear that I have no other lover than Haemon. If you like, I'll swear that I shall never have any other lover than Haemon. Save your tears, Nanny, save them, Nanny dear; you may still need them. When you cry like that, I become a little girl again; and I mustn't be a little girl today. (ANTIGONE *rises and moves upstage.*)

ISMENE *enters through arch, left. She pauses in front of arch.*

ISMENE. Antigone! What are you doing up at this hour? I've just been to your room.

NURSE. The two of you, now! You're both going mad, to be up before the kitchen fire has been started. Do you like running about without a mouthful of breakfast? Do you think it's decent for the daughters of a king? (*She turns to* ISMENE.) And look at you, with nothing on, and the sun not up! I'll have you both on my hands with colds before I know it.

ANTIGONE. Nanny dear, go away now. It's not chilly, really. Summer's here. Go and make us some coffee. Please, Nanny, I'd love some coffee. It would do me so much good.

NURSE. My poor baby! Her head's swimming, what with nothing on her stomach, and me standing here like an idiot when I could be getting her something hot to drink. (NURSE *exits.*)

A pause.

17

ISMENE. Aren't you well?

ANTIGONE. Of course I am. Just a little tired. I got up too early. (ANTIGONE *sits on a chair, suddenly tired.*)

ISMENE. I couldn't sleep, either.

ANTIGONE. Ismene, you ought not to go without your beauty sleep.

ISMENE. Don't make fun of me.

ANTIGONE. I'm not, Ismene, truly. This particular morning, seeing how beautiful you are makes everything easier for me. Wasn't I a miserable little beast when we were small? I used to fling mud at you, and put worms down your neck. I remember tying you to a tree and cutting off your hair. Your beautiful hair! How easy it must be never to be unreasonable with all that smooth silken hair so beautifully set round your head.

ISMENE (*abruptly*). Why do you insist upon talking about other things?

ANTIGONE (*gently*). I am not talking about other things.

ISMENE. Antigone, I've thought about it a lot.

ANTIGONE. Have you?

ISMENE. I thought about it all night long. Antigone, you're mad.

ANTIGONE. Am I?

ISMENE. We cannot do it.

ANTIGONE. Why not?

ISMENE. Creon will have us put to death.

ANTIGONE. Of course he will. That's what he's here for. He will do what he has to do, and we will do what we have to do. He is bound to put us to death. We are bound to go out and bury our brother. That's the way it is. What do you think we can do to change it?

ISMENE (*releases* ANTIGONE'S *hand; draws back a step*). I don't want to die.

ANTIGONE. I'd prefer not to die, myself.

18

ISMENE. Listen to me, Antigone. I thought about it all night. I'm older than you are. I always think things over, and you don't. You are impulsive. You get a notion in your head and you jump up and do the thing straight off. And if it's silly, well, so much the worse for you. Whereas, *I* think things out.

ANTIGONE. Sometimes it is better not to think too much.

ISMENE. I don't agree with you! (ANTIGONE *looks at* ISMENE, *then turns and moves to chair behind table.* ISMENE *leans on end of table top, towards* ANTIGONE.) Oh, I know it's horrible. And I pity Polynices just as much as you do. But all the same, I sort of see what Uncle Creon means.

ANTIGONE. I don't want to "sort of see" anything.

ISMENE. Uncle Creon is the king. He has to set an example!

ANTIGONE. But I am not the king; and I don't have to set people examples. Little Antigone gets a notion in her head—the nasty brat, the wilful, wicked girl; and they put her in a corner all day, or they lock her up in the cellar. And she deserves it. She shouldn't have disobeyed!

ISMENE. There you go, frowning, glowering, wanting your own stubborn way in everything. Listen to me, I'm right oftener than you are.

ANTIGONE. I don't want to be right!

ISMENE. At least you can try to understand.

ANTIGONE. Understand! The first word I ever heard out of any of you was the word "understand." Why didn't I "understand" that I must not play with water—cold, black, beautiful flowing water—because I'd spill it on the palace tiles. Or with earth, because earth dirties a little girl's frock. Why didn't I "understand" that nice children don't eat out of every dish at once; or give everything in their pockets to beggars; or run in the wind so fast that

19

they fall down; or ask for a drink when they're perspiring; or want to go swimming when it's either too early or too late, merely because they happen to feel like swimming. Understand! I don't want to understand. There'll be time enough to understand when I'm old. . . . If I ever *am* old. But not now.

ISMENE. He is stronger than we are, Antigone. He is the king. And the whole city is with him. Thousands and thousands of them, swarming through all the streets of Thebes.

ANTIGONE. I am not listening to you.

ISMENE. His mob will come running, howling as it runs. A thousand arms will seize our arms. A thousand breaths will breathe into our faces. Like one single pair of eyes, a thousand eyes will stare at us. We'll be driven in a tumbrel through their hatred, through the smell of them and their cruel, roaring laughter. We'll be dragged to the scaffold for torture, surrounded by guards with their idiot faces all bloated, their animal hands clean-washed for the sacrifice, their beefy eyes squinting as they stare at us. And we'll know that no shrieking and no begging will make them understand that we want to live, for they are like slaves who do exactly as they've been told, without caring about right or wrong. And we shall suffer, we shall feel pain rising in us until it becomes so unbearable that we *know* it must stop. But it won't stop; it will go on rising and rising, like a screaming voice. Oh, I can't, I can't, Antigone!

A pause.

ANTIGONE. How well you have thought it all out.
ISMENE. I thought of it all night long. Didn't you?
ANTIGONE. Oh, yes.
ISMENE. I'm an awful coward, Antigone.

20

ANTIGONE. So am I. But what has that to do with it?

ISMENE. But, Antigone! Don't you want to go on living?

ANTIGONE. Go on living! Who was it that was always the first out of bed because she loved the touch of the cold morning air on her bare skin? Who was always the last to bed because nothing less than infinite weariness could wean her from the lingering night? Who wept when she was little because there were too many grasses in the meadow, too many creatures in the field, for her to know and touch them all?

ISMENE (clasps ANTIGONE'S *hands, in a sudden rush of tenderness*). Darling little sister!

ANTIGONE (*repulsing her*). No! For heaven's sake! Don't paw me! And don't let us start snivelling! You say you've thought it all out. The howling mob—the torture—the fear of death. . . . They've made up your mind for you. Is that it?

ISMENE. Yes.

ANTIGONE. All right. They're as good excuses as any.

ISMENE. Antigone, be sensible. It's all very well for men to believe in ideas and die for them. But you are a girl!

ANTIGONE. Don't I know I'm a girl? Haven't I spent my life cursing the fact that I was a girl?

ISMENE (*with spirit*). Antigone! You have everything in the world to make you happy. All you have to do is reach out for it. You are going to be married; you are young; you are beautiful —

ANTIGONE. I am not beautiful.

ISMENE. Yes, you are! Not the way other girls are. But it's always you that the little boys turn to look back at when they pass us in the street. And when you go by, the little girls stop talking. They stare and stare at you, until we've turned a corner.

ANTIGONE (*a faint smile*). "Little boys—little girls."

ISMENE (*challengingly*). And what about Haemon?

A pause.

ANTIGONE. I shall see Haemon this morning. I'll take care
of Haemon. You always said I was mad; and it didn't
matter how little I was or what I wanted to do. Go back
to bed now, Ismene. The sun is coming up, and, as you
see, there is nothing I can do today. Our brother Polynices
is as well guarded as if he had won the war and were
sitting on his throne. Go along. You are pale with
weariness.

ISMENE. What are you going to do?

NURSE (*calls from off-stage*). Come along, my dove. Come
to breakfast.

ANTIGONE. I don't feel like going to bed. However, if you
like, I'll promise not to leave the house till you wake up.
Nurse is getting me breakfast. Go and get some sleep. The
sun is just up. Look at you: you can't keep your eyes
open. Go.

ISMENE. And you will listen to reason, won't you? You'll
let me talk to you about this again? Promise?

ANTIGONE. I promise. I'll let you talk. I'll let all of you
talk. Go to bed, now. (ISMENE *goes to arch and exits.*)
Poor Ismene!

NURSE (*enters through arch, speaking as she enters.*) Come
along, my dove. I've made you some coffee and toast and
jam. (*She turns towards arch as if to exit.*)

ANTIGONE. I'm not really hungry, Nurse.

   NURSE *stops, looks at* ANTIGONE, *then moves behind*
her.

NURSE (*very tenderly*). Where is your pain?

ANTIGONE. Nowhere, Nanny dear. But you must keep
me warm and safe, the way you used to do when I was

little. Nanny! Stronger than all fever, stronger than any nightmare, stronger than the shadow of the cupboard that used to snarl at me and turn into a dragon on the bedroom wall. Stronger than the thousand insects gnawing and nibbling in the silence of the night. Stronger than the night itself, with the weird hooting of the nightbirds that frightened me even when I couldn't hear them. Nanny, stronger than death, give me your hand, Nanny, as if I were ill in bed, and you sitting beside me.

NURSE. My sparrow, my lamb! What is it that's eating your heart out?

ANTIGONE. Oh, it's just that I'm a little young still for what I have to go through. But nobody but you must know that.

NURSE (*places her other arm round* ANTIGONE'S *shoulder*). A little young for what, my kitten?

ANTIGONE. Nothing in particular, Nanny. Just—all this. Oh, it's so good that you are here. I can hold your calloused hand, your hand that is so prompt to ward off evil. You are very powerful, Nanny.

NURSE. What is it you want me to do for you, my baby?

ANTIGONE. There isn't anything to do, except put your hand like this against my check. (*She places the* NURSE'S *hand against her cheek. A pause, then, as* ANTIGONE *leans back, her eyes shut.*) There! I'm not afraid any more. Not afraid of the wicked ogre, nor of the sandman, nor of the dwarf who steals little children. (*A pause.* ANTIGONE *resumes on another note.*) Nanny . . .

NURSE. Yes?

ANTIGONE. My dog, Puff . . .

NURSE (*straightens up, draws her hand away*). Well?

ANTIGONE. Promise me that you will never scold her again.

NURSE. Dogs that dirty up a house with their filthy paws deserve to be scolded.

ANTIGONE. I know. Just the same, promise me.

NURSE. You mean you want me to let her make a mess all over the place and not say a thing?

ANTIGONE. Yes, Nanny.

NURSE. You're asking a lot. The next time she wets my living-room carpet, I'll——

ANTIGONE. Please, Nanny, I beg of you!

NURSE. It isn't fair to take me on my weak side, just because you look a little peaked today. . . . Well, have it your own way. We'll mop up and keep our mouth shut. You're making a fool of me, though.

ANTIGONE. And promise me that you will talk to her. That you will talk to her often.

NURSE (*turns and looks at* ANTIGONE). Me, talk to a dog!

ANTIGONE. Yes. But mind you: you are not to talk to her the way people usually talk to dogs. You're to talk to her the way I talk to her.

NURSE. I don't see why both of us have to make fools of ourselves. So long as you're here, one ought to be enough.

ANTIGONE. But if there was a reason why I couldn't go on talking to her——

NURSE (*interrupting*). Couldn't go on talking to her! And why couldn't you go on talking to her? What kind of poppycock——?

ANTIGONE. And if she got too unhappy, if she moaned and moaned, waiting for me with her nose under the door as she does when I'm out all day, then the best thing, Nanny, might be to have her mercifully put to sleep.

NURSE. Now what *has* got into you this morning? (HAEMON *enters through arch*.) Running round in the darkness, won't sleep, won't eat—(ANTIGONE *sees* HAEMON) —and now it's her dog she wants killed. I never——

24

ANTIGONE (*interrupting*). Nanny! Haemon is here. Go inside, please. And don't forget that you've promised me. (NURSE *goes to arch and exits.* ANTIGONE *rises.*) Haemon, Haemon! Forgive me for quarrelling with you last night. (*She crosses quickly to* HAEMON *and they embrace.*) Forgive me for everything. It was all my fault. I beg you to forgive me.

HAEMON. You know that I've forgiven you. You had hardly slammed the door, your perfume still hung in the room, when I had already forgiven you. (*He holds her in his arms and smiles at her. Then draws slightly back.*) You stole that perfume. From whom?

ANTIGONE. Ismene.

HAEMON. And the rouge? and the face powder? and the frock? Whom did you steal them from?

ANTIGONE. Ismene.

HAEMON. And in whose honour did you get yourself up so elegantly?

ANTIGONE. I'll tell you everything. (*She draws him closer.*) Oh, darling, what a fool I was! To waste a whole evening! A whole, beautiful evening!

HAEMON. We'll have other evenings, my sweet.

ANTIGONE. Perhaps we won't.

HAEMON. And other quarrels, too. A happy love is full of quarrels, you know.

ANTIGONE. A happy love, yes. Haemon, listen to me.

HAEMON. Yes?

ANTIGONE. Don't laugh at me this morning. Be serious.

HAEMON. I am serious.

ANTIGONE. And hold me tight. Tighter than you have ever held me. I want all your strength to flow into me.

HAEMON. There! With all my strength.

   A pause.

ANTIGONE (*breathless*). That's good. (*They stand for a moment, silent and motionless.*) Haemon! I wanted to tell you. You know—the little boy we were going to have when we were married?

HAEMON. Yes?

ANTIGONE. I'd have protected him against everything in the world.

HAEMON. Yes, dearest.

ANTIGONE. Oh, you don't know how I should have held him in my arms and given him my strength. He wouldn't have been afraid of anything, I swear he wouldn't. Not of the falling night, nor of the terrible noonday sun, nor of all the shadows or all the walls in the world. Our little boy, Haemon! His mother wouldn't have been very imposing: her hair wouldn't always have been brushed; but she would have been strong where he was concerned, so much stronger than all those real mothers with their real bosoms and their aprons round their middle. You believe that, don't you, Haemon?

HAEMON (*soothingly*). Yes, yes, my darling.

ANTIGONE. And you believe me when I say that you would have had a real wife?

HAEMON. Darling, you are my real wife.

ANTIGONE (*pressing against him and crying out*). Haemon, you loved me! You did love me that night, didn't you? You're sure of it!

HAEMON (*rocking her gently*). What night, my sweet?

ANTIGONE. And you are very sure, aren't you, that that night, at the dance, when you came to the corner where I was sitting, there was no mistake? It was me you were looking for? It wasn't another girl? And you're sure that never, not in your most secret heart of hearts, have you said to yourself that it was Ismene you ought to have asked to marry you?

HAEMON (*reproachfully*). Antigone, you are idiotic. You might give me credit for knowing my own mind. It's you I love, and no one else.

ANTIGONE. But you love me as a woman—as a woman wants to be loved, don't you? Your arms round me aren't lying, are they? Your hands, so warm against my back—they're not lying? This warmth that's in me; this confidence, this sense that I am safe, secure, that flows through me as I stand here with my cheek in the hollow of your shoulder: they are not lies, are they?

HAEMON. Antigone, darling, I love you exactly as you love me. With all of myself.

They kiss.

ANTIGONE. I'm sallow, and I'm scrawny, Ismene is pink and golden. She's like a fruit.

HAEMON. Look here, Antigone——

ANTIGONE. Ah, dearest, I am ashamed of myself. But this morning, this special morning, I must know. Tell me the truth! I beg you to tell me the truth! When you think about me, when it strikes you suddenly that I am going to belong to you—do you have the feeling that—that a great empty space is being hollowed out inside you, that there is something inside you that is just—dying?

HAEMON. Yes, I do, I do.

A pause.

ANTIGONE. That's the way I feel. And another thing. I wanted you to know that I should have been very proud to be your wife—the woman whose shoulder you would put your hand on as you sat down to table, absent-mindedly, as upon a thing that belonged to you. (*After a moment, draws away from him. Her tone changes.*) There! Now I have two things more to tell you. And when I have told them to you, you must go away instantly, without asking any questions. However strange they may seem to you. However much they may hurt you. Swear that you will!

HAEMON (*beginning to be troubled*). What are these things that you are going to tell me?

ANTIGONE. Swear, first, that you will go away without one word. Without so much as looking at me. (*She looks at him, wretchedness in her face.*) You hear me, Haemon. Swear it, please. This is the last mad wish that you will ever have to grant me.

  A pause.

HAEMON. I swear it, since you insist. But I must tell you that I don't like this at all.

ANTIGONE. Please, Haemon. It's very serious. You must listen to me and do as I ask. First, about last night, when I came to your house. You asked me a moment ago why I wore Ismene's dress and rouge. It was because I was stupid. I wasn't very sure that you loved me as a woman; and I did it—because I wanted you to want me. I was trying to be more like other girls.

HAEMON. Was *that* the reason? My poor——

ANTIGONE. Yes. And you laughed at me. And we quarrelled; and my awful temper got the better of me and I flung out of the house. . . . The real reason was that I wanted you to take me; I wanted to be your wife before——

HAEMON. Oh, my darling——

ANTIGONE (*shuts him off*). You swore you wouldn't ask any questions. You swore, Haemon. (*Turns her face away and goes on in a hard voice.*) As a matter of fact, I'll tell you why. I wanted to be your wife last night because I love you that way very—very strongly. And also because—— Oh, my darling, my darling, forgive me; I'm going to

28

cause you quite a lot of pain. (*She draws away from him.*) I wanted it also because I shall never, never be able to marry you, never! (HAEMON *is stupefied and mute; then he moves a step towards her.*) Haemon! You took a solemn oath! You swore! Leave me quickly! Tomorrow the whole thing will be clear to you. Even before tomorrow: this afternoon. If you please, Haemon, go now. It is the only thing left that you can do for me if you still love me. (*A pause as* HAEMON *stares at her. Then he turns and goes out through the arch.* ANTIGONE *stands motionless, then moves to chair at end of table and lets herself gently down on it. In a mild voice, as of calm after storm.*) Well, it's over for Haemon, Antigone.

ISMENE *enters through arch, pauses for a moment in front of it when she sees* ANTIGONE, *then crosses behind table.*

ISMENE. I can't sleep. I'm terrified. I'm so afraid that even though it is daylight, you'll still try to bury Polynices. Antigone, little sister, we all want to make you happy—Haemon, and Nurse, and I, and Puff whom you love. We love you, we are alive, we need you. And you remember what Polynices was like. He was our brother, of course. But he's dead; and he never loved you. He was a bad brother. He was like an enemy in the house. He never thought of you. Why should you think of him? What if his soul does have to wander through endless time without rest or peace? Don't try something that is beyond your strength. You are always defying the world, but you're only a girl, after all. Stay at home tonight. Don't try to do it, I beg you. It's Creon's doing, not ours.

ANTIGONE. You are too late, Ismene. When you first saw me this morning, I had just come in from burying him.

(ANTIGONE *exits through arch.*)

The lighting, which by this time has reached a point of early morning sun, is quickly dimmed out, leaving the stage bathed in a light blue colour.

ISMENE *runs out after* ANTIGONE.

On ISMENE'S *exit the lights are brought up suddenly to suggest a later period of the day.*

CREON *and* PAGE *enter through curtain upstage.* CREON *stands on the top step; his* PAGE *stands at his right side.*

CREON. A private of the guards, you say? One of those standing watch over the body? Show him in.

The PAGE *crosses to arch and exits.* CREON *moves down to end of table.*

PAGE *re-enters, preceded by the* FIRST GUARD, *livid with fear.* PAGE *remains on upstage side of arch.* GUARD *salutes.*

GUARD. Private Jonas, Second Battalion.
CREON. What are you doing here?
GUARD. It's like this, sir. Soon as it happened, we said: "Got to tell the chief about this before anybody else spills it. He'll want to know right away." So we tossed a coin to see which one would come up and tell you about it. You see, sir, we thought only one man had better come because, after all, you don't want to leave the body without a guard. Right? I mean, there's three of us on duty, guarding the body.
CREON. What's wrong about the body?
GUARD. Sir, I've been seventeen years in the service. Volunteer. Wounded three times. Two mentions. My record's clean. I know my business and I know my place.

30

I carry out orders. Sir, ask any officer in the battalion; they'll tell you. "Leave it to Jonas. Give him an order: he'll carry it out." That's what they'll tell you, sir. Jonas, that's me—that's my name.

CREON. What's the matter with you, man? What are you shaking for?

GUARD. By rights it's the corporal's job, sir. I've been recommended for a corporal but they haven't put it through yet. June, it was supposed to go through.

CREON (*interrupts*). Stop chattering and tell me why you are here. If anything has gone wrong, I'll break all three of you.

GUARD. Nobody can say we didn't keep our eye on that body. We had the two o'clock watch—the tough one. You know how it is, sir. It's nearly the end of the night. Your eyes are like lead. You've got a crick in the back of your neck. There's shadows, and the fog is beginning to roll in. A fine watch they give us! And me, seventeen years in the service. But we was doing our duty all right. On our feet, all of us. Anybody says we were sleeping is a liar. First place, it was too cold. Second place—— (CREON *makes a gesture of impatience*.) Yes, sir. Well, I turned round and looked at the body. We wasn't only ten feet away from it, but that's how I am. I was keeping my eye on it. (*Shouts.*) Listen, sir, I was the first man to see it! Me! They'll tell you. I was the one let out that yell!

CREON. What for? What was the matter?

GUARD. Sir, the body! Somebody had been there and buried it. (CREON *comes down a step on the stair. The* GUARD *becomes more frightened*.) It wasn't much, you understand. With us three there, it couldn't have been. Just covered over with a little dirt, that's all. But enough to hide it from the buzzards.

31

CREON. By God, I'll——! (*He looks intently at the* GUARD.)
You are sure that it couldn't have been a dog, scratching
up the earth?

GUARD. Not a chance, sir. That's kind of what we
hoped it was. But the earth was scattered over
the body just like the priests tell you you should do it.
Whoever did that job knew what he was doing all
right.

CREON. Who could have dared? (*He turns and looks at the*
GUARD.) Was there anything to indicate who might have
done it?

GUARD. Not a thing, sir. Maybe we heard a footstep—
I can't swear to it. Of course we started right in to search,
and the corporal found a shovel, a kid's shovel, no
bigger than that, all rusty and everything. Corporal's
got the shovel for you. We thought maybe a kid
did it.

CREON (*to himself*). A kid! (*He looks away from the* GUARD.)
I broke the back of the rebellion; but like a snake, it is
coming together again. Polynices' friends, with their
gold, blocked by my orders in the banks of Thebes. The
leaders of the mob, stinking of garlic and allied to envious
princes. And the temple priests, always ready for a bit of
fishing in troubled waters. A kid! I can imagine what he is
like, their kid: a baby-faced killer, creeping in the night
with a toy shovel under his jacket. (*He looks at his* PAGE.)
Though why shouldn't they have corrupted a real child?
Very touching! Very useful to the party, an innocent child.
A martyr. A real white-faced baby of fourteen who will
spit with contempt at the guards who kill him. A free gift
to their cause: the precious, innocent blood of a child on
my hands. (*He turns to the* GUARD.) They must have
accomplices in the Guard itself. Look here, you. Who
knows about this?

32

GUARD. Only us three, sir. We flipped a coin, and I came right over.

CREON. Right. Listen, now. You will continue on duty. When the relief squad comes up, you will tell them to return to barracks. You will uncover the body. If another attempt is made to bury it, I shall expect you to make an arrest and bring the person straight to me. And you will keep your mouths shut. Not one word of this to a human soul. You are all guilty of neglect of duty, and you will be punished; but if the rumour spreads through Thebes that the body received burial, you will be shot—all three of you.

GUARD (*excitedly*). Sir, we never told anybody, I swear we didn't! Anyhow, I've been up here. Suppose my pals spilled it to the relief; I couldn't have been with them and here too. That wouldn't be my fault if they talked. Sir, I've got two kids. You're my witness, sir, it couldn't have been me. I was here with you. I've got a witness! If anybody talked, it couldn't have been me! I was——

CREON (*interrupting*). Clear out! If the story doesn't get round, you won't be shot. (*The* GUARD *salutes, turns and exits, at the double.* CREON *turns and paces upstage, then comes down to end of the table.*) A child! (*He looks at* PAGE.) Come along, my lad. Since we can't hope to keep this to ourselves, we shall have to be the first to give out the news. And after that, we shall have to clean up the mess. (*PAGE crosses to side of* CREON. CREON *puts his hand on* PAGE'S *shoulder.*) Would you be willing to die for me? Would you defy the Guard with your little shovel? (*PAGE looks up at* CREON.) Of course you would. You would do it, too. (*A pause.* CREON *looks away from* PAGE *and murmurs*) A child! (CREON *and* PAGE *go slowly upstage centre to top step.* PAGE *draws aside the curtain, through which* CREON *exits with* PAGE *behind him.*)

As soon as CREON *and* PAGE *have disappeared,* CHORUS
*enters and leans against the upstage portal of arch, left.
The lighting is brought up to its brightest point to suggest mid-afternoon.* CHORUS *allows a pause to indicate
that a crucial moment has been reached in the play,
then moves slowly downstage, centre. He stands
for a moment silent, reflecting, and then smiles
faintly.*

CHORUS. The spring is wound up tight. It will uncoil of
itself. That is what is so convenient in tragedy. The least
little turn of the wrist will do the job. Anything will set it
going: a glance at a girl who happens to be lifting her arms
to her hair as you go by; a feeling when you wake up on a
fine morning that you'd like a little respect paid to you today, as if it were as easy to order as a second cup of coffee;
one question too many, idly thrown out over a friendly
drink—and the tragedy is on.
The rest is automatic. You don't need to lift a finger. The
machine is in perfect order, it has been oiled ever since
time began, and it runs without friction. Death, treason
and sorrow are on the march; and they move in the wake
of storm, of tears, of stillness. Every kind of stillness. The
hush when the executioner's axe goes up at the end of the
last act. The unbreathable silence when, at the beginning
of the play, the two lovers, their hearts bared, their bodies
naked, stand for the first time face to face in the darkened
room, afraid to stir. The silence inside you when the roaring crowd acclaims the winner—so that you think of a
film without a sound-track, mouths agape and no sound
coming out of them, a clamour that is no more than a
picture; and you, the victor, already vanquished, alone in
the desert of your silence. That is tragedy.
Tragedy is clean, it is restful, it is flawless. It has nothing

34

to do with melodrama—with wicked villains, persecuted maidens, avengers, sudden revelations and eleventh-hour repentances. Death, in a melodrama, is really horrible because it is never inevitable. The dear old father might so easily have been saved; the honest young man might so easily have brought in the police five minutes earlier.

In a tragedy, nothing is in doubt and everyone's destiny is known. That makes for tranquillity. There is a sort of fellow-feeling among characters in a tragedy: he who kills is as innocent as he who gets killed: it's all a matter of what part you are playing. Tragedy is restful; and the reason is that hope, that foul, deceitful thing, has no part in it. There isn't any hope. You're trapped. The whole sky has fallen on you, and all you can do about it is to shout. Don't mistake me: I said "shout": I did not say groan, whimper, complain. That, you cannot do. But you can shout aloud; you can get all those things said that you never thought you'd be able to say—or never even knew you had it in you to say. And you don't say these things because it will do any good to say them: you know better than that. You say them for their own sake; you say them because you learn a lot from them.

In melodrama, you argue and struggle in the hope of escape. That is vulgar; it's practical. But in tragedy, where there is no temptation to try to escape, argument is gratuitous: it's kingly.

Voices of the GUARDS *and scuffling sounds heard through the archway.* CHORUS *looks in that direction, then, in a changed tone.*

The play is on. Antigone has been caught. For the first time in her life, little Antigone is going to be able to be herself.

CHORUS *exits through arch.*

A pause, while the offstage voices rise in volume, then the FIRST GUARD *enters, followed by* SECOND *and* THIRD GUARDS, *holding the arms of* ANTIGONE *and dragging her along. The* FIRST GUARD, *speaking as he enters, crosses swiftly to end of the table. The* TWO GUARDS *and* ANTIGONE *stop downstage.*

FIRST GUARD (*recovered from his fright*). Come on, now, Miss, give it a rest. The chief will be here in a minute and you can tell him about it. All I know is my orders. I don't want to know what you were doing there. People always have excuses; but I can't afford to listen to them, see. Why, if we had to listen to all the people who want to tell us what's the matter with this country, we'd never get our work done. (*To the* GUARDS.) You keep hold of her and I'll see that she keeps her face shut.

ANTIGONE. They are hurting me. Tell them to take their dirty hands off me.

FIRST GUARD. Dirty hands, eh? The least you can do is try to be polite, Miss. Look at me: I'm polite.

ANTIGONE. Tell them to let me go. I shan't run away. My father was King Oedipus. I am Antigone.

FIRST GUARD. King Oedipus' little girl! Well, well, well! Listen, Miss, the night watch never picks up a lady but they say, you better be careful: I'm sleeping with the police commissioner.

The GUARDS *laugh.*

ANTIGONE. I don't mind being killed, but I don't want them to touch me.

FIRST GUARD. And what about stiffs, and dirt, and such like? You wasn't afraid to touch them, was you? "Their dirty hands!" Take a look at your own hands. (ANTIGONE,

36

handcuffed, smiles despite herself as she looks down at her hands. They are grubby.) You must have lost your shovel, didn't you? Had to go at it with your fingernails the second time, I'll bet. By God, I never saw such nerve! I turn my back for about five seconds; I ask a pal for a chew; I say "thanks"; I get the tobacco stowed away in my cheek—the whole thing don't take ten seconds; and there she is, clawing away like a hyena. Right out in broad daylight! And did she scratch and kick when I grabbed her! Straight for my eyes with them nails she went. And yelling something fierce about, "I haven't finished yet; let me finish!" She ain't got all her marbles!

SECOND GUARD. I pinched a nut like that the other day. Right on the main square she was, hoisting up her skirts and showing her behind to anybody that wanted to take a look.

FIRST GUARD. Listen, we're going to get a bonus out of this. What do you say we throw a party, the three of us?

SECOND GUARD. At the old woman's? Behind Market Street?

THIRD GUARD. Suits me. Sunday would be a good day. We're off duty Sunday. What do you say we bring our wives?

FIRST GUARD. No. Let's have some fun this time. Bring your wife, there's always something goes wrong. First place, what do you do with the kids? Bring them, they always want to go to the can just when you're right in the middle of a game of cards or something. Listen, who would have thought an hour ago that us three would be talking about throwing a party now? The way I felt when the old man was interrogating me, we'd be lucky if we got off with being docked a month's pay. I want to tell you, I was scared.

37

SECOND GUARD. You sure we're going to get a bonus?

FIRST GUARD. Yes. Something tells me this is big stuff.

THIRD GUARD (*to* SECOND GUARD). What's-his-name, you know—in the Third Battalion? He got an extra month's pay for catching a fire-bug.

SECOND GUARD. If we get an extra month's pay, I vote we throw the party at the Arabian's.

FIRST GUARD. You're crazy! He charges twice as much for liquor as anybody else in town. Unless you want to go upstairs, of course. Can't do that at the old woman's.

THIRD GUARD. Well, we can't keep this from our wives, no matter how you work it out. You get an extra month's pay, and what happens? Everybody in the battalion knows it, and your wife knows it too. They might even line up the battalion and give it to you in front of everybody, so how could you keep your wife from finding out?

FIRST GUARD. Well, we'll see about that. If they do the job out in the barrack-yard—of course that means women, kids, everything.

ANTIGONE. I should like to sit down, if you please.

A pause, as the FIRST GUARD *thinks it over.*

FIRST GUARD. Let her sit down. But keep hold of her. (*The two* GUARDS *start to lead her towards the chair at end of table. The curtain upstage opens, and* CREON *enters, followed by his* PAGE. FIRST GUARD *turns and moves upstage a few steps, sees* CREON.) 'Tenshun! (*The three* GUARDS *salute.* CREON, *seeing* ANTIGONE *handcuffed to* THIRD GUARD, *stops on the top step, astonished.*)

CREON. Antigone! (*To the* FIRST GUARD.) Take off those handcuffs! (FIRST GUARD *crosses above table to left of* ANTIGONE.) What is this? (CREON *and his* PAGE *come down off the steps.*)

38

FIRST GUARD *takes key from his pocket and unlocks the cuff on* ANTIGONE'S *hand.* ANTIGONE *rubs her wrist as she crosses below table towards chair at end of table.* SECOND *and* THIRD GUARDS *step back to front of arch.* FIRST GUARD *turns upstage towards* CREON.

FIRST GUARD. The watch, sir. We all came this time.

CREON. Who is guarding the body?

FIRST GUARD. We sent for the relief.

CREON *comes down.*

CREON. But I gave orders that the relief was to go back to barracks and stay there! (ANTIGONE *sits on chair at left of table.*) I told you not to open your mouth about this!

FIRST GUARD. Nobody's said anything, sir. We made this arrest, and brought the party in, the way you said we should.

CREON (*to* ANTIGONE). Where did these men find you?

FIRST GUARD. Right by the body.

CREON. What were you doing near your brother's body? You knew what my orders were.

FIRST GUARD. What was she doing? Sir, that's why we brought her in. She was digging up the dirt with her nails. She was trying to cover up the body all over again.

CREON. Do you realize what you are saying?

FIRST GUARD. Sir, ask these men here. After I reported to you, I went back, and first thing we did, we uncovered the body. The sun was coming up and it was beginning to smell, so we moved it up on a little rise to get him in the wind. Of course, you wouldn't expect any trouble in broad daylight. But just the same, we decided one of us had better keep his eye peeled all the time. About noon, what with the sun and the smell, and as the wind dropped and I wasn't feeling none too good, I went over to my pal

39

to get a chew. I just had time to say "thanks" and stick it in my mouth, when I turned round and there she was, clawing away at the dirt with both hands. Right out in broad daylight! Wouldn't you think when she saw me come running she'd stop and leg it out of there? Not her! She went right on digging as fast as she could, as if I wasn't there at all. And when I grabbed her, she scratched and bit and yelled to leave her alone, she hadn't finished yet, the body wasn't all covered yet, and the like of that.

CREON (*to* ANTIGONE). Is this true?

ANTIGONE. Yes, it is true.

FIRST GUARD. We scraped the dirt off as fast as we could, then we sent for the relief and we posted them. But we didn't tell them a thing, sir. And we brought in the party so's you could see her. And that's the truth, so help me God.

CREON (*to* ANTIGONE). And was it you who covered the body the first time? In the night?

ANTIGONE. Yes, it was. With a toy shovel we used to take to the seashore when we were children. It was Polynices' own shovel; he had cut his name in the handle. That was why I left it with him. But these men took it away; so the next time, I had to do it with my hands.

FIRST GUARD. Sir, she was clawing away like a wild animal. Matter of fact, first minute we saw her, what with the heat haze and everything, my pal says, "That must be a dog," he says. "Dog!" I says. "That's a girl, that is!" And it was.

CREON. Very well. (*Turns to the* PAGE.) Show these men to the ante-room. (*The* PAGE *crosses to the arch, stands there, waiting.* CREON *moves behind the table. To the* FIRST GUARD.) You three men will wait outside. I may want a report from you later.

FIRST GUARD. Do I put the cuffs back on her, sir?

40

CREON. No. (*The three* GUARDS *salute, do an about-turn and exit through arch, right.* PAGE *follows them out. A pause.*) Had you told anybody what you meant to do?

ANTIGONE. No.

CREON. Did you meet anyone on your way—coming or going?

ANTIGONE. No, nobody.

CREON. Sure of that, are you?

ANTIGONE. Perfectly sure.

CREON. Very well. Now listen to me. You will go straight to your room. When you get there, you will go to bed. You will say that you are not well and that you have not been out since yesterday. Your nurse will tell the same story. (*He looks towards arch, through which the* GUARDS *have exited.*) And I'll get rid of those three men.

ANTIGONE. Uncle Creon, you are going to a lot of trouble for no good reason. You must know that I'll do it all over again tonight.

A pause. They look one another in the eye.

CREON. Why did you try to bury your brother?

ANTIGONE. I owed it to him.

CREON. I had forbidden it.

ANTIGONE. I owed it to him. Those who are not buried wander eternally and find no rest. If my brother were alive, and he came home weary after a long day's hunting, I should kneel down and unlace his boots, I should fetch him food and drink, I should see that his bed was ready for him. Polynices is home from the hunt. I owe it to him to unlock the house of the dead in which my father and my mother are waiting to welcome him. Polynices has earned his rest.

CREON. Polynices was a rebel and a traitor, and you know it.

41

ANTIGONE. He was my brother.

CREON. You heard my edict. It was proclaimed through-
out Thebes. You read my edict. It was posted up on the
city walls.

ANTIGONE. Of course I did.

CREON. You knew the punishment I decreed for any
person who attempted to give him burial.

ANTIGONE. Yes, I knew the punishment.

CREON. Did you by any chance act on the assumption that
a daughter of Oedipus, a daughter of Oedipus' stubborn
pride, was above the law?

ANTIGONE. No, I did not act on that assumption.

CREON. Because if you had acted on that assumption,
Antigone, you would have been deeply wrong. Nobody
has a more sacred obligation to obey the law than those
who make the law. You are a daughter of law-makers, a
daughter of kings, Antigone. You must observe the
law.

ANTIGONE. Had I been a scullery maid washing my dishes
when that law was read aloud to me, I should have
scrubbed the greasy water from my arms and gone out in
my apron to bury my brother.

CREON. What nonsense! If you had been a scullery maid,
there would have been no doubt in your mind about the
seriousness of that edict. You would have known that it
meant death; and you would have been satisfied to weep
for your brother in your kitchen. But you! You thought
that because you come of the royal line, because you were
my niece and were going to marry my son, I shouldn't
dare have you killed.

ANTIGONE. You are mistaken. Quite the contrary. I never
doubted for an instant that you would have me put to
death.

A pause, as CREON *stares fixedly at her.*

CREON. The pride of Oedipus! Oedipus and his head-strong pride all over again. I can see your father in you—and I believe you. Of course you thought that I should have you killed! Proud as you are, it seemed to you a natural climax in your existence. Your father was like that. For him as for you human happiness was meaningless; and mere human misery was not enough to satisfy his passion for torment. (*He sits on stool behind the table.*) You come of people for whom the human vestment is a kind of straitjacket: it cracks at the seams. You spend your lives wriggling to get out of it. Nothing less than a cosy tea party with death and destiny will quench your thirst. The happiest hour of your father's life came when he listened greedily to the story of how, unknown to him-self, he had killed his own father and dishonoured the bed of his own mother. Drop by drop, word by word, he drank in the dark story that the gods had destined him, first to live and then to hear. How avidly men and women drink the brew of such a tale when their names are Oedipus—and Antigone! And it is so simple, afterwards, to do what your father did, to put out one's eyes and take one's daughter begging on the highways.

Let me tell you, Antigone: those days are over for Thebes. Thebes has a right to a king without a past. My name, thank God, is only Creon. I stand here with both feet firm on the ground; with both hands in my pockets; and I have decided that so long as I am king—being less ambitious than your father was—I shall merely devote myself to introducing a little order into this absurd kingdom; if that is possible.

Don't think that being a king seems to me romantic. It is my trade; a trade a man has to work at every day; and like every other trade, it isn't all beer and skittles. But since it is my trade, I take it seriously. And if, tomorrow, some wild and bearded messenger walks in from some wild and distant valley—which is what happened to your dad—and tells me that he's not quite sure who my parents were, but thinks that my wife Eurydice is actually my mother, I shall ask him to do me the kindness to go back where he came from; and I shan't let a little matter like that persuade me to order my wife to take a blood test and the police to let me know whether or not my birth certificate was forged. Kings, my girl, have other things to do than to surrender themselves to their private feelings. (*He looks at her and smiles.*) Hand *you* over to be killed! (*He rises, moves to end of table and sits on the top of table.*) I have other plans for you. You're going to marry Haemon; and I want you to fatten up a bit so that you can give him a sturdy boy. Let me assure you that Thebes needs that boy a good deal more than it needs your death. You will go to your room, now, and do as you have been told; and you won't say a word about this to anybody. Don't fret about the guards: I'll see that their mouths are shut. And don't annihilate me with those eyes. I know that you think I am a brute, and I'm sure you must consider me very prosaic. But the fact is, I have always been fond of you, stubborn though you always were. Don't forget that the first doll you ever had came from me. (*A pause.* ANTIGONE *says nothing, rises and crosses slowly below the table towards the arch.* CREON *turns and watches her; then*) Where are you going?

ANTIGONE (*stops downstage. Without any show of rebellion*). You know very well where I am going.

CREON (*after a pause*). What sort of game are you playing?

ANTIGONE. I am not playing games.

CREON. Antigone, do you realize that if, apart from those three guards, a single soul finds out what you have tried to do, it will be impossible for me to avoid putting you to death? There is still a chance that I can save you; but only if you keep this to yourself and give up your crazy purpose. Five minutes more, and it will be too late. You understand that?

ANTIGONE. I must go and bury my brother. Those men uncovered him.

CREON. What good will it do? You know that there are other men standing guard over Polynices. And even if you did cover him over with earth again, the earth would again be removed.

ANTIGONE. I know all that. I know it. But that much, at least, I can do. And what a person can do, a person ought to do.

Pause.

CREON. Tell me, Antigone, do you believe all that flummery about religious burial? Do you really believe that a so-called shade of your brother is condemned to wander for ever homeless if a little earth is not flung on his corpse to the accompaniment of some priestly abracadabra? Have you ever listened to the priests of Thebes when they were mumbling their formula? Have you ever watched those dreary bureaucrats while they were preparing the dead for burial—skipping half the gestures required by the ritual, swallowing half their words, hustling the dead into their graves out of fear that they might be late for lunch?

ANTIGONE. Yes, I have seen all that.

CREON. And did you never say to yourself as you watched them, that if someone you really loved lay dead under the shuffling, mumbling ministrations of the priests, you would scream aloud and beg the priests to leave the dead in peace?

ANTIGONE. Yes, I've thought all that.

CREON. And you still insist upon being put to death—merely because I refuse to let your brother go out with

45

that grotesque passport; because I refuse his body the wretched consolation of that mass-production jibber-jabber, which you would have been the first to be embarrassed by if I had allowed it. The whole thing is absurd!

ANTIGONE. Yes, it's absurd.

CREON. Then, why, Antigone, why? For whose sake? For the sake of them that believe in it? To raise them against me?

ANTIGONE. No.

CREON. For whom then if not for them and not for Polynices either?

ANTIGONE. For nobody. For myself.

A pause as they stand looking at one another.

CREON. You must want very much to die. You look like a trapped animal.

ANTIGONE. Stop feeling sorry for me. Do as I do. Do your job. But if you are a human being, do it quickly. That is all I ask of you. I'm not going to be able to hold out for ever.

CREON (*takes a step towards her*). I want to save you, Antigone.

ANTIGONE. You are the king, and you are all-powerful. But that you cannot do.

CREON. You think not?

ANTIGONE. Neither save me nor stop me.

CREON. Prideful Antigone! Little Oedipus!

ANTIGONE. Only this can you do: have me put to death.

CREON. Have you tortured, perhaps?

ANTIGONE. Why would you do that? To see me cry? To hear me beg for mercy? Or swear whatever you wish, and then begin over again?

A pause.

46

CREON. You listen to me. You have cast me for the villain in this little play of yours, and yourself for the heroine. And you know it, you damned little mischief-maker! But don't you drive me too far! If I were one of your preposterous little tyrants that Greece is full of, you would be lying in a ditch this minute with your tongue pulled out and your body drawn and quartered. But you can see something in my face that makes me hesitate to send for the guards and turn you over to them. Instead, I let you go on arguing; and you taunt me, you take the offensive. (*He grasps her left wrist.*) What are you driving at, you she-devil?

ANTIGONE. Let me go. You are hurting my arm.

CREON (*gripping her tighter*). I will not let you go.

ANTIGONE (*moans*). Oh!

CREON. I was a fool to waste words. I should have done this from the beginning. (*He looks at her.*) I may be your uncle—but we are not a particularly affectionate family. Are we, eh? (*Through his teeth, as he twists.*) Are we? (CREON *propels* ANTIGONE *round below him to his side.*) What fun for you, eh? To be able to spit in the face of a king who has all the power in the world; a man who has done his own killing in his day; who has killed people just as pitiable as you are—and who is still soft enough to go to all this trouble in order to keep you from being killed.

A pause.

ANTIGONE. Now you are squeezing my arm too tightly. It doesn't hurt any more.

CREON *stares at her, then drops her arm.*

CREON. I shall save you yet. (*He goes below the table at the chair at end of table, takes off his coat and places it on the chair.*) God knows, I have things enough to do today without

47

wasting my time on an insect like you. There's plenty to do, I assure you, when you've just put down a revolution. But urgent things can wait. I am not going to let politics be the cause of your death. For it is a fact that this whole business is nothing but politics: the mournful shade of Polynices, the decomposing corpse, the sentimental weeping and the hysteria that you mistake for heroism—nothing but politics.

Look here. I may not be soft, but I'm fastidious. I like things clean, ship-shape, well scrubbed. Don't think that I am not just as offended as you are by the thought of that meat rotting in the sun. In the evening, when the breeze comes in off the sea, you can smell it in the palace, and it nauseates me. But I refuse even to shut my window. It's vile; and I can tell you what I wouldn't tell anybody else: it's stupid, monstrously stupid. But the people of Thebes have got to have their noses rubbed into it a little longer. My God! If it was up to me, I should have had them bury your brother long ago as a mere matter of public hygiene. I admit that what I am doing is childish. But if the featherheaded rabble I govern are to understand what's what, that stench has got to fill the town for a month!

ANTIGONE (*turns to him*). You are a loathsome man!

CREON. I agree. My trade forces me to be. We could argue whether I ought or ought not to follow my trade; but once I take on the job, I must do it properly.

ANTIGONE. Why do you do it at all?

CREON. My dear, I woke up one morning and found myself King of Thebes. God knows, there were other things I loved in life more than power.

ANTIGONE. Then you should have said no.

CREON. Yes, I could have done that. Only, I felt that it would have been cowardly. I should have been like a

48

workman who turns down a job that has to be done. So I said yes.

ANTIGONE. So much the worse for you, then. I didn't say yes. I can say no to anything I think vile, and I don't have to count the cost. But because you said yes, all that you can do, for all your crown and your trappings, and your guards—all that you can do is to have me killed.

CREON. Listen to me.

ANTIGONE. If I want to. I don't have to listen to you if I don't want to. You've said your *yes*. There is nothing more you can tell me that I don't know. You stand there, drinking in my words. (*She moves behind chair.*) Why is it that you don't call your guards? I'll tell you why. You want to hear me out to the end; that's why.

CREON. You amuse me.

ANTIGONE. Oh, no, I don't. I frighten you. That is why you talk about saving me. Everything would be so much easier if you had a docile, tongue-tied little Antigone living in the palace. I'll tell you something, Uncle Creon: I'll give you back one of your own words. You are too fastidious to make a good tyrant. But you are going to have to put me to death today, and you know it. And that's what frightens you. God! Is there anything uglier than a frightened man!

CREON. Very well. I am afraid, then. Does that satisfy you? I am afraid that if you insist upon it, I shall have to have you killed. And I don't want to.

ANTIGONE. I don't have to do things that I think are wrong. If it comes to that, you didn't really want to leave my brother's body unburied, did you? Say it! Admit that you didn't.

CREON. I have said it already.

49

ANTIGONE. But you did it just the same. And now, though you don't want to do it, you are going to have me killed. And you call that being a king!

CREON. Yes, I call that being a king.

ANTIGONE. Poor Creon! My nails are broken, my fingers are bleeding, my arms are covered with the welts left by the paws of your guards—but I am a queen!

CREON. Then why not have pity on me, and live? Isn't your brother's corpse, rotting there under my windows, payment enough for peace and order in Thebes? My son loves you. Don't make me add your life to the payment. I've paid enough.

ANTIGONE. No, Creon! You said yes, and made yourself king. Now you will never stop paying.

CREON. But God in Heaven! Won't you try to understand me! I'm trying hard enough to understand you! There had to be one man who said yes. Somebody had to agree to captain the ship. She had sprung a hundred leaks; she was loaded to the water-line with crime, ignorance, poverty. The wheel was swinging with the wind. The crew refused to work and were looting the cargo. The officers were building a raft, ready to slip overboard and desert the ship. The mast was splitting, the wind was howling, the sails were beginning to rip. Every man-jack on board was about to drown—and only because the only thing they thought of was their own skins and their cheap little day-to-day traffic. Was that a time, do you think, for playing with words like yes and no? Was that a time for a man to be weighing the pros and cons, wondering if he wasn't going to pay too dearly later on; if he wasn't going to lose his life, or his family, or his touch with other men? You grab the wheel, you right the ship in the face of a mountain of water. You shout an order, and if one man refuses to obey, you shoot straight into the mob. Into the mob, I say! The beast as nameless as the wave that crashes down upon your deck; as nameless as the whipping wind. The thing that drops when you shoot may be someone who poured you a drink the night before; but it has no name. And you, braced at the wheel, you have no name, either. Nothing has a name—except the ship, and the storm. (*A pause as he looks at her.*) Now do you understand?

ANTIGONE. I am not here to understand. That's all very well for you. I am here to say no to you, and die.

CREON. It is easy to say no.

ANTIGONE. Not always.

CREON. It is easy to say no. To say yes, you have to sweat and roll up your sleeves and plunge both hands into life up to the elbows. It is easy to say no, even if saying no means death. All you have to do is to sit still and wait. Wait to go on living; wait to be killed. That is the coward's part. *No* is one of your man-made words. Can you imagine a world in which trees say *no* to the sap? In which beasts say *no* to hunger or to propagation? Animals are good, simple, tough. They move in droves, nudging one another onwards, all travelling the same road. Some of them keel over; but the rest go on; and no matter how many may fall by the wayside, there are always those few left which go on bringing their young into the world, travelling the same road with the same obstinate will, unchanged from those who went before.

ANTIGONE. Animals, eh, Creon! What a king you could be if only men were animals!

A pause. CREON *turns and looks at her.*

CREON. You despise me, don't you? (ANTIGONE *is silent.* CREON *goes on, as if to himself.*) Strange. Again and again, I have imagined myself holding this conversation with a pale young man I have never seen in the flesh. He would have come to assassinate me, and would have failed. I would be trying to find out from him why he wanted to kill me. But with all my logic and all my powers of debate, the only thing I could get out of him would be that he despised me. Who would have thought that the white-faced boy would turn out to be you? And that the debate would arise out of something so meaningless as the burial of your brother?

ANTIGONE (*repeats contemptuously*). Meaningless!

CREON (*earnestly, almost desperately*). And yet, you must hear me out. My part is not an heroic one, but I shall play my part. I shall have you put to death. Only, before I do, I want to make one last appeal. I want to be sure that you know what you are doing as well as I know what I am doing. Antigone, do you know what you are dying for? Do you know the sordid story to which you are going to sign your name in blood, for all time to come?

ANTIGONE. What story?

CREON. The story of Eteocles and Polynices, the story of your brothers. You think you know it, but you don't. Nobody in Thebes knows that story but me. And it seems to me, this afternoon, that you have a right to know it too. (*A pause as* ANTIGONE *moves to chair and sits*). It's not a pretty story. (*He turns, gets stool from behind the table and places it between the table and the chair.*) You'll see. (*He looks at her for a moment.*) Tell me, first. What do you remember about your brothers? They were older than you, so they must have looked down on you. And I imagine that they tormented you—pulled your pigtails, broke your dolls, whispered secrets to each other to put you in a rage.

ANTIGONE. They were big and I was little.

CREON. And later on, when they came home wearing evening clothes, smoking cigarettes, they would have nothing to do with you; and you thought they were wonderful.

ANTIGONE. They were boys and I was a girl.

CREON. You know why, exactly, but you knew that they were making your mother unhappy. You saw her in tears over them; and your father would fly into a rage because of them. You heard them come in, slamming doors, laughing noisily in the corridors—insolent, spineless, unruly, smelling of drink.

ANTIGONE (*staring outward*). Once, it was very early and we had just got up. I saw them coming home, and hid behind a door. Polynices was very pale and his eyes were shining. He was so handsome in his evening clothes. He saw me, and said: "Here, this is for you"; and he gave me a big paper flower that he had brought home from his night out.

CREON. And of course you still have that flower. Last night, before you crept out, you opened a drawer and looked at it for a time, to give yourself courage.

ANTIGONE. Who told you so?

CREON. Poor Antigone! With her night-club flower. Do you know what your brother was?

ANTIGONE. Whatever he was, I know that you will say vile things about him.

CREON. A cheap, idiotic bounder, that is what he was. A cruel, vicious little voluptuary. A little beast with just wit enough to drive a car faster and throw more money away than any of his pals. I was with your father one day when Polynices, having lost a lot of money gambling, asked him to settle the debt; and when your father refused, the boy raised his hand against him and called him a vile name.

ANTIGONE. That's a lie!

CREON. He struck your father in the face with his fist. It was pitiful. Your father sat at his desk with his head in his

53

hands. His nose was bleeding. He was weeping with anguish. And in a corner of your father's study, Polynices stood sneering and lighting a cigarette.

ANTIGONE. That's a lie.

A pause.

CREON. When did you last see Polynices alive? When you were twelve years old. *That's* true, isn't it?

ANTIGONE. Yes, that's true.

CREON. Now you know why. Oedipus was too chicken-hearted to have the boy locked up. Polynices was allowed to go off and join the Argive army. And as soon as he reached Argos, the attempts upon your father's life began —upon the life of an old man who couldn't make up his mind to die, couldn't bear to be parted from his kingship. One after another, men slipped into Thebes from Argos for the purpose of assassinating him, and every killer we caught always ended by confessing who had put him up to it, who had paid him to try it. And it wasn't only Polynices. That is really what I am trying to tell you. I want you to know what went on in the backroom, in the kitchen of politics; I want you to know what took place in the wings of this drama in which you are burning to play a part.

Yesterday, I gave Eteocles a State funeral, with pomp and honours. Today, Eteocles is a saint and a hero in the eyes of all Thebes. The whole city turned out to bury him. The schoolchildren emptied their savings-boxes to buy wreaths for him. Old men, orating in quavering, hypocritical voices, glorified the virtue of the great-hearted brother, the devoted son, the loyal prince. I made a speech myself; and every temple priest was present with an appropriate show of sorrow and solemnity in his stupid face. And military honours were accorded the dead hero.

Well, what else could I have done? People had taken sides

in the civil war. Both sides couldn't be wrong; that would be too much. I couldn't have made them swallow the truth. Two gangsters was more of a luxury than I could afford. (*He pauses for a moment.*) And this is the whole point of my story. Eteocles, that virtuous brother, was just as rotten as Polynices. That great-hearted son had done his best, too, to procure the assassination of his father. That loyal prince had also offered to sell out Thebes to the highest bidder.

Funny, isn't it? Polynices lies rotting in the sun while Eteocles is given a hero's funeral and will be housed in a marble vault. Yet I have absolute proof that everything that Polynices did, Eteocles had plotted to do. They were a pair of blackguards—both engaged in selling out Thebes, and both engaged in selling out each other; and they died like the cheap gangsters they were, over a division of the spoils.

But, as I told you a moment ago, I had to make a martyr of one of them. I sent out to the holocaust for their bodies; they were found clasped in one another's arms—for the first time in their lives, I imagine. Each had been spitted on the other's sword, and the Argive cavalry had trampled them down. They were mashed to a pulp, Antigone. I had the prettier of the two carcasses brought in, and gave it a State funeral; and I left the other to rot. I don't know which was which. And I assure you, I don't care. (*Long silence, neither looking at the other.*)

ANTIGONE (*in a mild voice*). Why do you tell me all this?

CREON. Would it have been better to let you die a victim to that obscene story?

ANTIGONE. It might have been. I had my faith.

CREON. What are you going to do now?

ANTIGONE (*rises to her feet in a daze*). I shall go up to my room.

CREON. Don't stay alone. Go and find Haemon. And get married quickly.

ANTIGONE (*in a whisper*). Yes.

CREON. All this is really beside the point. You have your whole life ahead of you—and life is a treasure.

ANTIGONE. Yes.

CREON. And you were about to throw it away. Don't think me fatuous if I say that I understand you; and that at your age I should have done the same thing. A moment ago, when we were quarrelling, you said I was drinking in your words. I was. But it wasn't you I was listening to; it was a lad named Creon who lived here in Thebes many years ago. He as thin and pale as you are. His mind, too, was filled with thoughts of self-sacrifice. Go and find Haemon. And get married quickly, Antigone. Be happy. Life flows like water, and you young people let it run away through your fingers. Shut your hands; hold on to it, Antigone. Life is not what you think it is. Life is a child playing round your feet, a tool you hold firmly in your grip, a bench you sit down upon in the evening, in your garden. People will tell you that that's not life, that life is something else. They will tell you that because they need your strength and your fire, and they will want to make use of you. Don't listen to them. Believe me, the only poor consolation that we have in our old age is to discover that what I have just said to you is true. Life is nothing more than the happiness that you get out of it.

ANTIGONE (*murmurs, lost in thought*). Happiness . . .

CREON (*suddenly a little self-conscious*). Not much of a word, is it?

ANTIGONE (*quietly*). What kind of happiness do you foresee for me? Paint me the picture of your happy Antigone. What are the unimportant little sins that I shall have to commit before I am allowed to sink my teeth into life and tear happiness from it? Tell me: to whom shall I have to lie? Upon whom shall I have to fawn? To whom must I sell myself? Whom do you want me to leave dying, while I turn away my eyes?

CREON. Antigone, be quiet.

ANTIGONE. Why do you tell me to be quiet when all I want to know is what I have to do to be happy? This minute; since it is this very minute that I must make my choice. You tell me that life is so wonderful. I want to know what I have to do in order to be able to say that myself.

CREON. Do you love Haemon?

ANTIGONE. Yes, I love Haemon. The Haemon I love is hard and young, faithful and difficult to satisfy, just as I am. But if what I love in Haemon is to be worn away like a stone step by the tread of the thing you call life, the thing you call happiness; if Haemon reaches the point where he stops growing pale with fear when I grow pale, stops thinking that I must have been killed in an accident when I am five minutes late, stops feeling that he is alone on earth when I laugh and he doesn't know why—if he too has to learn to say yes to everything—why, no, then, no! I do not love Haemon!

CREON. You don't know what you are talking about!

ANTIGONE. I do know what I am talking about! Now it is you who have stopped understanding. I am too far away from you now, talking to you from a kingdom you can't get into, with your quick tongue and your hollow heart. (*Laughs.*) I laugh, Creon, because I see you suddenly as you must have been at fifteen: the same look of impotence in your face and the same inner conviction that there was nothing you couldn't do. What has life added to you, except those lines in your face, and that fat on your stomach?

CREON. Be quiet, I tell you!

ANTIGONE. Why do you want me to be quiet? Because you know that I am right? Do you think I can't see in your face that what I am saying is true? You can't admit it, of course; you have to go on growling and defending the bone you call happiness.

CREON. It is your happiness, too, you little fool!

ANTIGONE. I spit on your happiness! I spit on your idea of life—that life that must go on, come what may. You are all like dogs that lick everything they smell. You with your promise of a humdrum happiness—provided a person doesn't ask too much of life. I want everything of life, I do; and I want it now! I want it total, complete: otherwise I reject it! I will *not* be moderate. I will *not* be satisfied with the bit of cake you offer me if I promise to be a good little girl. I want to be sure of everything this very day; sure that everything will be as beautiful as when I was a little girl. If not, I want to die!

CREON. Scream on, daughter of Oedipus! Scream on, in your father's own voice!

ANTIGONE. In my father's own voice, yes! We are of the tribe that asks questions, and we ask them to the bitter end. Until no tiniest chance of hope remains to be strangled by our hands. We are of the tribe that hates your filthy hope, your docile, female hope; hope, your whore——

CREON (*grasps her by her arms*). Shut up! If you could see how ugly you are, shrieking those words!

ANTIGONE. Yes, I am ugly! Father was ugly, too. (CREON *releases her arms, turns and moves away. Stands with his back to* ANTIGONE.) But Father became beautiful. And do you know when? (*She follows him to behind the table.*) At the very end. When all his questions had been answered. When he could no longer doubt that he *had* killed his own father; that he *had* gone to bed with his own mother.

When all hope was gone, stamped out like a beetle. When it was absolutely certain that nothing, nothing could save him. Then he was at peace; then he could smile, almost; then he became beautiful. . . . Whereas you! Ah, those faces of yours, you candidates for election to happiness! It's you who are the ugly ones, even the handsomest of you—with that ugly glint in the corner of your eyes, that ugly crease at the corner of your mouths. Creon, you spoke the word a moment ago: the kitchen of politics. You look it and you smell of it.

CREON (*struggles to put his hand over her mouth*). I order you to shut up! Do you hear me!

ANTIGONE. *You* order me? Cook! Do you really believe that you can give me orders?

CREON. Antigone! The ante-room is full of people! Do you want them to hear you?

ANTIGONE. Open the doors! Let us make sure that they can hear me!

CREON. By God! You shut up, I tell you!

ISMENE *enters through arch.*

ISMENE (*distraught*). Antigone!

ANTIGONE (*turns to* ISMENE). You, too? What do you want?

ISMENE. Oh, forgive me, Antigone. I've come back. I'll be brave. I'll go with you now.

ANTIGONE. Where will you go with me?

ISMENE (*to* CREON). Creon! If you kill her, you'll have to kill me too.

ANTIGONE. Oh, no, Ismene. Not a bit of it. I die alone. You don't think I'm going to let you die with me after what I've been through? You don't deserve it.

ISMENE. If you die, I don't want to live. I don't want to be left behind, alone.

59

ANTIGONE. You chose life and I chose death. Now stop blubbering. You had your chance to come with me in the black night, creeping on your hands and knees. You had your chance to claw up the earth with your nails, as I did; to get yourself caught like a thief, as I did. And you refused it.

ISMENE. Not any more. I'll do it alone tonight.

ANTIGONE (*turns round towards* CREON). You hear that, Creon? The thing is catching! Who knows but that lots of people will catch the disease from me! What are you waiting for? Call in your guards! Come on, Creon! Show a little courage! It only hurts for a minute! Come on, cook!

CREON (*turns towards arch and calls*). Guard!

GUARDS *enter through arch.*

ANTIGONE (*in a great cry of relief*). At last, Creon!

CHORUS *enters through left arch.*

CREON (*to the* GUARDS). Take her away! (CREON *goes up on top step.*)

GUARDS *grasp* ANTIGONE *by her arms, turn and hustle her towards the arch, right, and exit.*

ISMENE *mimes horror, backs away towards the arch, left, then turns and runs out through the arch.*
A long pause, as CREON *moves slowly downstage.*

CHORUS (*behind* CREON. *Speaks in a deliberate voice*). You are out of your mind, Creon. What have you done?

CREON (*his back to* CHORUS). She had to die.

CHORUS. You must not let Antigone die. We shall carry the scar of her death for centuries.

CREON. She insisted. No man on earth was strong enough to dissuade her. Death was her purpose, whether she knew it or not. Polynices was a mere pretext. When she had to give up that pretext, she found another one—that life and happiness were tawdry things and not worth possessing. She was bent upon only one thing: to reject life and to die.

CHORUS. She is a mere child, Creon.

CREON. What do you want me to do for her? Condemn her to live?

HAEMON (*calls from offstage*). Father! (HAEMON *enters through arch, right.* CREON *turns towards him.*)

CREON. Haemon, forget Antigone. Forget her, my dearest boy.

HAEMON. How can you talk like that?

CREON (*grasps* HAEMON *by the hands*). I did everything I could to save her, Haemon. I used every argument. I swear I did. The girl doesn't love you. She could have gone on living for you; but she refused. She wanted it this way; she wanted to die.

HAEMON. Father! The guards are dragging Antigone away! You've got to stop them! (*He breaks away from* CREON.)

CREON (*looks away from* HAEMON). I can't stop them. It's too late. Antigone has spoken. The story is all over Thebes. I cannot save her now.

CHORUS. Creon, you must find a way. Lock her up. Say that she has gone out of her mind.

CREON. Everybody will know it isn't so. The nation will say that I am making an exception of her because my son loves her. I cannot.

CHORUS. You can still gain time, and get her out of Thebes.

CREON. The mob already knows the truth. It is howling for her blood. I can do nothing.

HAEMON. But, Father, you are master in Thebes!

CREON. I am master under the law. Not above the law.

HAEMON. You cannot let Antigone be taken from me. I am your son!

CREON. I cannot do anything else, my poor boy. She must die and you must live.

HAEMON. Live, you say! Live a life without Antigone? A life in which I am to go on admiring you as you busy yourself about your kingdom, make your persuasive speeches, strike your attitudes? Not without Antigone. I love Antigone. I will not live without Antigone!

CREON. Haemon—you will have to resign yourself to life without Antigone. (*He moves to left of* HAEMON.) Sooner or later there comes a day of sorrow in each man's life when he must cease to be a child and take up the burden of manhood. That day has come for you.

HAEMON (*backs away a step*). That giant strength, that courage. That massive god who used to pick me up in his arms and shelter me from shadows and monsters—was that you, Father? Was it of you I stood in awe? Was that man you?

CREON. For God's sake, Haemon, do not judge me! Not you, too!

HAEMON (*pleading now*). This is all a bad dream, Father. You are not yourself. It isn't true that we have been backed up against a wall, forced to surrender. We don't have to say *yes* to this terrible thing. You are still king. You are still the father I revered. You have no right to desert me, to shrink into nothingness. The world will be too bare, I shall be too alone in the world, if you force me to disown you.

CREON. The world *is* bare, Haemon, and you *are* alone. You must cease to think your father all-powerful. Look straight at me. See your father as he is. That is what it means to grow up and be a man.

62

HAEMON (*stares at* CREON *for a moment*). I tell you that I will not live without Antigone. (*Turns and goes quickly out through arch.*)

CHORUS. Creon, the boy will go mad.

CREON. Poor boy! He loves her.

CHORUS. Creon, the boy is wounded to death.

CREON. We are all wounded to death.

> FIRST GUARD *enters through arch, right, followed by* SECOND *and* THIRD GUARDS *pulling* ANTIGONE *along with them.*

FIRST GUARD. Sir, the people are crowding into the palace!

ANTIGONE. Creon, I don't want to see their faces. I don't want to hear them howl. You are going to kill me; let that be enough. I want to be alone until it is over.

CREON. Empty the palace! Guards at the gates! (CREON *quickly crosses towards the arch and exits. Two* GUARDS *release* ANTIGONE *and exit behind* CREON. CHORUS *goes out through arch, left.*)

> *The lighting dims so that only the area about the table is lighted. The cyclorama is covered with a dark blue colour. The scene is intended to suggest a prison cell, filled with shadows and dimly lit.*

> ANTIGONE *moves to stool and sits. The* FIRST GUARD *stands upstage. He watches* ANTIGONE, *and as she sits, he begins pacing slowly downstage, then upstage.*

> *A pause.*

ANTIGONE (*turns and looks at the* GUARD). It's you, is it?

GUARD. What do you mean, me?

ANTIGONE. The last human face that I shall see. (*A pause as they look at each other, then* GUARD *paces upstage;*

63

turns and crosses behind table.) Was it you that arrested me this morning?

GUARD. Yes, that was me.

ANTIGONE. You hurt me. There was no need for you to hurt me. Did I act as if I was trying to escape?

GUARD. Come on now, Miss. It was my business to bring you in. I did it. (*A pause. He paces to and fro upstage. Only the sound of his boots is heard.*)

ANTIGONE. How old are you?

GUARD. Thirty-nine.

ANTIGONE. Have you any children?

GUARD. Yes. Two.

ANTIGONE. Do you love your children?

GUARD. What's that got to do with you? (*A pause. He paces upstage and downstage.*)

ANTIGONE. How long have you been in the Guard?

GUARD. Since the war. I was in the army. Sergeant. Then I joined the Guard.

ANTIGONE. Does one have to have been an army sergeant to get into the Guard?

GUARD. Supposed to be. Either that or on special detail. But when they make you a guard, you lose your stripes.

ANTIGONE (*murmurs*). I see.

GUARD. Yes. Of course, if you're a guard, everybody knows you're something special; they know you're an old N.C.O. Take pay, for instance. When you're a guard you get your pay, and on top of that you get six months' extra pay, to make sure you don't lose anything by not being a sergeant any more. And of course you do better than that. You get a house, coal, rations, extras for the wife and kids. If you've got two kids, like me, you draw better than a sergeant.

ANTIGONE (*barely audible*). I see.

GUARD. That's why sergeants, now, they don't like

64

guards. Maybe you noticed they try to make out they're better than us? Promotion, that's what it is. In the army, anybody can get promoted. All you need is good conduct. Now in the Guard, it's slow, and you have to know your business—like how to make out a report and the like of that. But when you're an N.C.O. in the Guard, you've got something that even a sergeant-major ain't got. For instance——

ANTIGONE (*breaking him off*). Listen.

GUARD. Yes, Miss.

ANTIGONE. I'm going to die soon.

> The GUARD *looks at her for a moment, then turns and* moves away.

GUARD. For instance, people have a lot of respect for guards, they have. A guard may be a soldier, but he's kind of in the civil service, too.

ANTIGONE. Do you think it hurts to die?

GUARD. How would I know? Of course, if some-body sticks a sabre in your guts and turns it round, it hurts.

ANTIGONE. How are they going to put me to death?

GUARD. Well, I'll tell you. I heard the proclamation all right. Wait a minute. How did it go now? (*He stares into space and recites from memory.*) "In order that our fair city shall not be pol-luted with her sinful blood, she shall be im-mured—immured." That means, they shove you in a cave and wall up the cave.

ANTIGONE. Alive?

GUARD. Yes. . . . (*He moves away a few steps.*)

ANTIGONE (*murmurs*). O tomb! O bridal bed! Alone! (ANTIGONE *sits there, a tiny figure in the middle of the stage. You would say she felt a little chilly. She wraps her arms round herself.*)

GUARD. Yes! Outside the south-east gate of the town. In the Cave of Hades. In broad daylight. Some detail, eh, for them that's on the job! First they thought maybe it was a job for the army. Now it looks like it's going to be the Guard. There's an outfit for you! Nothing the Guard can't do. No wonder the army's jealous.

ANTIGONE. A pair of animals.

GUARD. What do you mean, a pair of animals?

ANTIGONE. When the winds blow cold, all they need do is to press close against one another. I am all alone.

GUARD. Is there anything you want? I can send out for it, you know.

ANTIGONE. You are very kind. (*A pause.* ANTIGONE *looks up at the* GUARD.) Yes, there is something I want. I want you to give someone a letter from me, when I am dead.

GUARD. How's that again? A letter?

ANTIGONE. Yes, I want to write a letter; and I want you to give it to someone for me.

GUARD (*straightens up*). Now, wait a minute. Take it easy. It's as much as my job is worth to go handing out letters from prisoners.

ANTIGONE (*removes a ring from her finger and holds it out towards him*). I'll give you this ring if you will do it.

GUARD. Is it gold? (He takes the ring from her.)

ANTIGONE. Yes, it is gold.

GUARD (*shakes his head*). Uh-uh. No can do. Suppose they go through my pockets. I might get six months for a thing like that. (*He stares at the ring, then glances off right to make sure that he is not being watched.*) Listen, tell you what I'll do. You tell me what you want to say, and I'll write it down in my book. Then, afterwards, I'll tear out the pages and give them to the party, see? If it's in my handwriting, it's all right.

ANTIGONE (*winces*). In your handwriting? (*She shudders slightly.*) No. That would be awful. The poor darling! In your handwriting.

GUARD (*offers back the ring*). O.K. It's no skin off my nose.

ANTIGONE (*quickly*). Of course, of course. No, keep the ring. But hurry. Time is getting short. Where is your note-book? (*The* GUARD *pockets the ring, takes his notebook and pencil from his pocket, puts his foot up on chair, and rests the notebook on his knee, licks his pencil.*) Ready? (*He nods.*) Write, now. "My darling . . ."

GUARD (*writes as he mutters*). The boy friend, eh?

ANTIGONE. "My darling. I wanted to die, and perhaps you will not love me any more . . ."

GUARD (*mutters as he writes*) ". . . will not love me any more."

ANTIGONE. "Creon was right. It is terrible to die."

GUARD (*repeats as he writes*) ". . . terrible to die."

ANTIGONE. "And I don't even know what I am dying for. I am afraid . . ."

GUARD (*looks at her*). Wait a minute! How fast do you think I can write?

ANTIGONE (*takes hold of herself*). Where are you?

GUARD (*reads from his notebook*). "And I don't even know what I am dying for."

ANTIGONE. No. Scratch that out. Nobody must know that. They have no right to know. It's as if they saw me naked and touched me, after I was dead. Scratch it all out. Just write: "Forgive me."

GUARD (*looks at* ANTIGONE). I cut out everything you said there at the end, and I put down, "Forgive me"?

ANTIGONE. Yes. "Forgive me, my darling. You would all have been so happy except for Antigone. I love you."

GUARD (*finishes the letter*) ". . . I love you." (*He looks at her.*) Is that all?

ANTIGONE. That's all.

GUARD (*straightens up, looks at notebook*). Damn funny letter.

ANTIGONE. I know.

GUARD (*looks at her*). Who is it to? (*A sudden roll of drums begins and continues until after* ANTIGONE *exits. The* FIRST GUARD *pockets the notebook and shouts at* ANTIGONE.) O.K. That's enough out of you! Come on!

> At the sound of the drum roll, SECOND *and* THIRD GUARDS *enter through the right arch.* ANTIGONE *rises.* GUARDS *seize her and exit with her.*

> *The lighting moves up to suggest late afternoon.*

> CHORUS *enters.*

CHORUS. And now it is Creon's turn.

> MESSENGER *runs through the arch, right.*

MESSENGER. The Queen . . . the Queen! Where is the Queen?

CHORUS. What do you want with the Queen? What have you to tell the Queen?

MESSENGER. News to break her heart. Antigone had just been thrust into the cave. They hadn't finished heaving the last blocks of stone into place when Creon and the rest heard a sudden moaning from the tomb. A hush fell over us all, for it was not the voice of Antigone. It was Haemon's voice that came forth from the tomb. Everybody looked at Creon; and he howled like a man demented: "Take away the stones! Take away the stones!" The slaves leaped at the wall of stones, and Creon worked with them, sweating and tearing at the blocks with his

68

bleeding hands. Finally a narrow opening was forced, and into it slipped the smallest guard.

Antigone had hanged herself by the cord of her robe, by the red and golden twisted cord of her robe. The cord was round her neck like a child's collar. Haemon was on his knees, holding her in his arms and moaning, his face buried in her robe. More stones were removed, and Creon went into the tomb. He tried to raise Haemon to his feet. I could hear him begging Haemon to rise to his feet. Haemon was deaf to his father's voice, till suddenly he stood up of his own accord, his eyes dark and burning. Anguish was in his face, but it was the face of a little boy. He stared at his father. Then suddenly he struck him—hard; and he drew his sword. Creon leaped out of range. Haemon went on staring at him, his eyes full of contempt—a glance that was like a knife, and that Creon couldn't escape. The King stood trembling in the far corner of the tomb, and Haemon went on staring. Then, without a word, he stabbed himself and lay down beside Antigone, embracing her in a great pool of blood.

A pause as CREON *and* PAGE *enter through arch on the* MESSENGER'S *last words.* CHORUS *and the* MESSENGER *both turn to look at* CREON, *then the* MESSENGER *exits through curtain.*

CREON. I have had them laid out side by side. They are together at last, and at peace. Two lovers on the morrow of their bridal. Their work is done.

CHORUS. But not yours, Creon. You have still one thing to learn. Eurydice, the Queen, your wife——

CREON. A good woman. Always busy with her garden, her preserves, her jerseys—those jerseys she never stopped knitting for the poor. Strange, how the poor never stop

needing jerseys. One would almost think that was all they
needed.

CHORUS. The poor in Thebes are going to be cold this
winter, Creon. When the Queen was told of her son's
death, she waited carefully until she had finished her row,
then put down her knitting calmly—as she did everything.
She went up to her room, her lavender-scented room, with
its embroidered doilies and its pictures framed in plush;
and there, Creon, she cut her throat. She is laid out now
in one of those two old-fashioned twin beds, exactly
where you went to her one night when she was still a
maiden. Her smile is still the same, scarcely a shade more
melancholy. And if it were not for that great red blot on
the bed linen by her neck, one might think she was asleep.

CREON (*in a dull voice*). She, too. They are all asleep.
(*Pause.*) It must be good to sleep.

CHORUS. And now you are alone, Creon.

CREON. Yes, all alone. (*To* PAGE.) My lad.

PAGE. Sir?

CREON. Listen to me. They don't know it, but the truth is
the work is there to be done, and a man can't fold his
arms and refuse to do it. They say it's dirty work. But if
we didn't do it, who would?

PAGE. I don't know, sir.

CREON. Of course you don't. You'll be lucky if you never
find out. In a hurry to grow up, aren't you?

PAGE. Oh yes, sir.

CREON. I shouldn't be if I were you. Never grow up if you
can help it. (*He is lost in thought as the hour chimes.*)
What time is it?

PAGE. Five o'clock, sir.

CREON. What have we on at five o'clock?

PAGE. Cabinet meeting, sir.

CREON. Cabinet meeting. Then we had better go along to it.

CREON *and* PAGE *exit slowly through arch, left, and* CHORUS *moves downstage.*

CHORUS. And there we are. It is quite true that if it had not been for Antigone they would all have been at peace. But that is over now. And they are all at peace. All those who were meant to die have died: those who believed one thing, those who believed the contrary thing, and even those who believed nothing at all, yet were caught up in the web without knowing why. All dead: stiff, useless, rotting. And those who have survived will now begin quietly to forget the dead: they won't remember who was who or which was which. It is all over. Antigone is calm tonight and we shall never know the name of the fever that consumed her. She has played her part.

Three GUARDS *enter, resume their places on steps as at the rise of the curtain, and begin to play cards.*

A great melancholy wave of peace now settled down upon Thebes, upon the empty palace, upon Creon, who can now begin to wait for his own death.
Only the guards are left, and none of this matters to them. It's no skin off their noses. They go on playing cards.

CHORUS *walks towards the arch, left, as*

THE CURTAIN FALLS

METHUEN MODERN PLAYS

include work by

Jean Anouilh
John Arden
Margaretta D'Arcy
Peter Barnes
Brendan Behan
Edward Bond
Bertolt Brecht
Howard Brenton
Jim Cartwright
Caryl Churchill
Noël Coward
Sarah Daniels
Shelagh Delaney
David Edgar
Dario Fo
Michael Frayn
John Guare
Peter Handke
Terry Johnson
Kaufman & Hart
Barrie Keeffe
Larry Kramer
Stephen Lowe

Doug Lucie
John McGrath
David Mamet
Arthur Miller
Mtwa, Ngema & Simon
Tom Murphy
Peter Nichols
Joe Orton
Louise Page
Luigi Pirandello
Stephen Poliakoff
Franca Rame
David Rudkin
Willy Russell
Jean-Paul Sartre
Sam Shepard
Wole Soyinka
C. P. Taylor
Theatre Workshop
Sue Townsend
Timberlake Wertenbaker
Victoria Wood

METHUEN WORLD CLASSICS

Aeschylus (two volumes)
Jean Anouilh
John Arden
Arden & D'Arcy
Aristophanes (two volumes)
Peter Barnes
Brendan Behan
Aphra Behn
Edward Bond (four volumes)
Bertolt Brecht (three volumes)
Howard Brenton (two volumes)
Büchner
Bulgakov
Calderón
Anton Chekhov
Caryl Churchill (two volumes)
Noël Coward (five volumes)
Sarah Daniels
Eduardo De Filippo
David Edgar (three volumes)
Euripides (three volumes)
Dario Fo
Michael Frayn (two volumes)
Max Frisch
Gorky
Harley Granville Barker
Henrik Ibsen (six volumes)

Lorca (three volumes)
Marivaux
Mustapha Matura
David Mercer
Arthur Miller (three volumes)
Anthony Minghella
Molière
Tom Murphy (two volumes)
Peter Nichols (two volumes)
Clifford Odets
Joe Orton
Louise Page
A. W. Pinero
Luigi Pirandello
Stephen Poliakoff
Terence Rattigan (two volumes)
Ntozake Shange
Sophocles (two volumes)
Wole Soyinka
David Storey
August Strindberg
    (three volumes)
J. M. Synge
Ramón del Valle-Inclán
Frank Wedekind
Oscar Wilde